Learn About Rural Life

Life in a Mining Community

Natalie Hyde

Crabtree Publishing Company

www.crabtreebooks.com

Author: Natalie Hyde
Editor-in-Chief: Lionel Bender
Editors: Simon Adams and Molly Aloian
Proofreader: Crystal Sikkens
Editorial director: Kathy Middleton
Photo research: Natalie Hyde and Ben White
Designer: Ben White
Production coordinator: Katherine Berti
Production: Kim Richardson
Prepress technician: Margaret Amy Salter
Consultant: Heather L. Montgomery, DragonFly
    Environmental Education Programs

Front cover (main image): An aerial view of the
    Black Thunder surface coal mine near Wright,
    Wyoming, U.S.A.
Back cover: New pine trees grow on reclaimed land
    that was once a mine.
Title page: A coal-removal truck in operation
    at a mine near Wright, Wyoming, U.S.A.

This book was produced for Crabtree Publishing
Company by Bender Richardson White.

Photographs and reproductions
Alamy: Jeff Morgan tourism and leisure: front cover
    (inset); Jim Harvey: front cover (main image)
BigStockPhoto: p. 26
Corbis Images: Jonathan Blair: p. 16; Karen
    Kasmauski/Science Faction: p. 25
Getty Images: AFP: p. 27, 29; Bruce Forster: p. 6;
    National Geographic: back cover, p. 11, 23, 24; Robert
    Nickelsburg: p. 18, 19, 20, 21, 22
High Plains Sentinel newspaper, Wright:
    Noahleh Olsen: p. 14, 17; Noleen Wright: p. 15
Istockphoto: page corner graphic, p. 1, 4, 5, 7, 8, 9, 28
Meghan and Tuffy Ferguson: p. 12, 13
Topfoto: The Granger Collection: p. 10

Acknowledgments
Special thanks to:
Meghan Ferguson of Wright, and to Noahleh Olsen of
High Plains Sentinel newspaper, for providing images
and information about Wright.

Library and Archives Canada Cataloguing in Publication

Hyde, Natalie, 1963-
    Life in a mining community / Natalie Hyde.

(Learn about rural life)
Includes index.
ISBN 978-0-7787-5074-1 (bound).--ISBN 978-0-7787-5087-1 (pbk.)

        1. Mineral industries--Juvenile literature. 2. Miners--Juvenile
literature. 3. Wright (Wyo.)--Juvenile literature. 4. Hedley
(B.C.)--Juvenile literature. I. Title. II. Series: Learn about
rural life

TN148.H93 2009   j622   C2009-903740-8

Library of Congress Cataloging-in-Publication Data

Hyde, Natalie, 1963-
    Life in a mining community / Natalie Hyde.
        p. cm. -- (Learn about rural life)
    Includes index.
    ISBN 978-0-7787-5087-1 (pbk. : alk. paper) -- ISBN 978-0-7787-
5074-1 (reinforced library binding : alk. paper)
    1. Miners--North America--Social conditions--Juvenile literature.
2. North America--Rural conditions--Juvenile literature. 3.
Mineral industries--North America--Juvenile literature. I. Title. II.
Series.

TN148.H93 2009
622.097--dc22

2009023639

Crabtree Publishing Company

www.crabtreebooks.com   1-800-387-7650

**Published
in Canada**
Crabtree Publishing
616 Welland Ave.
St. Catharines, Ontario
L2M 5V6

**Published in
the United States**
Crabtree Publishing
PMB16A
350 Fifth Ave., Suite 3308
New York, NY 10118

**Published in the
United Kingdom**
Crabtree Publishing
White Cross Mills
High Town, Lancaster
LA1 4XS

**Published
in Australia**
Crabtree Publishing
386 Mt. Alexander Rd.
Ascot Vale (Melbourne)
VIC 3032

Contents

A Rural Mining Town

Most people live in big **towns** or **cities**. These are busy, noisy places where everything and everyone moves fast. Big towns and cities are called **urban** places. Other people live in small towns and **villages**. Here, everyday life is quieter and slower. There are fewer people and fewer buildings. Small towns and villages are known as **rural** places.

▼ Large urban areas, such as Chicago in the United States, contain millions of people living and working together.

Hedley, a rural mining town in a valley in British Columbia, Canada, was settled by miners looking for gold in the mountains.

People need the same **resources** or basic things no matter where they live. They need food and clean water. They need a place to live and **energy** for their homes and vehicles. They need jobs to earn money. Rural places are built close to these resources. This book looks at Wright, a small, rural **mining** town in Wyoming, United States.

Types of Mines

Minerals, such as diamonds and **coal**, occur naturally in the earth. People removed them from the earth in **mines**. There are two types of mines—surface and underground. **Surface mines** are just big holes dug in the ground.

▼ Miners at this mine in South Africa work very deep underground to dig gold from hard rock.

At this surface mine in Arizona, mineral containing valuable copper is close to the surface of the earth. Rock containing the mineral is just scraped or dug away to get at the copper.

Underground mines are full of **tunnels** that follow a band of minerals or rock through the ground. Some of the deepest mines are cut 10,000 feet (3,030 meters) down into the earth. They can be dangerous because the ground can collapse and trap miners. At all mines, **explosives** are used to loosen rock so the valuable mineral can be removed.

Minerals and Ores

Many types of minerals are mined. Diamonds are the hardest material on Earth. They are hard enough to use on the tips of drills and saws. A diamond tip can cut through almost anything. Diamonds are also used in jewelry. An **ore** is a mineral containing **metal**. Iron ore is used to make steel. We use steel to build houses and to make vehicles.

▼ In this steel plant, iron ore is first melted in a furnace or huge oven, to free the iron. The hot, liquid iron is poured into molds, or shapes, and left to cool.

Coal is an important source of energy. Coal-fired power plants make the power that turns on our lights and heats many of our homes.

Metals such as copper, nickel, and silver can be used to make coins. They can also be **recycled** or used again. The mine where the metal came from cannot be reused. As more mineral or rock is dug up, the mine becomes empty. Coal is also gone forever once it has been burned for energy.

Mining in North America

Mining on a big scale started in the 1800s. Coal was used for energy. Clay was dug from the earth to make bricks. Today, copper is used to make water pipes, iron is used to make steel, and aluminum is used to make drink and food cans.

▼ During the Klondike gold rush more than 100 years ago, thousands of people moved to Dawson City in the Yukon to mine for gold.

Miners in the Northwest Territories of Canada use large pans to find diamonds in river beds. The pans collect little pieces of rocks and minerals washed up by the river.

Mines in North America helped open up rural areas. People who came to mine stayed and built towns. Mining brings money to many areas and provides many different jobs for people. The Inuit people live in northern Canada. There are diamond mines on their native lands. Many people who work in the diamond mines are Inuit.

Welcome to Wright

Wright is a small, rural **community** in Wyoming. If you look on an old map, you will not even find the town marked. Wright did not exist before 1976. The town was built for the workers of the nearby coal mines. At first, people in Wright lived in mobile homes. No houses had yet been built. The town had only one elementary school, a few stores, and some other buildings.

▼ Wright is built on the rolling grasslands of Wyoming. The next town is about 35 miles (56 km) away.

There are playgrounds, parks, a baseball field, a fishing pond, a golf course, and trails for people to enjoy in Wright.

The coal mines provided steady jobs that paid good wages, so Wright grew quickly. New homes were built on streets named after the countryside, such as Sweetwater Circle and Prairieview Drive. The town soon added a high school, a library, and a post office. There was enough money to build a new **recreation center** with an indoor swimming pool.

Daily Life

Most adults work at mines outside Wright or in small stores and offices in the town. When children are not in school, they play soccer, football, baseball, basketball, or practice track and field events. Some do karate, gymnastics, or dance. Because Wright is small, people often walk around town— there is no public transportation.

▼ There are many ranches that form part of Wright. On ranches, cowboys use horses to round up cattle.

Many people spend time fishing at Panther Pond in Wright. They also watch the buffalo that live on a ranch close to the pond.

The pool in the recreation center is a great place to learn to swim. The swim team has had members who have gone on to try out for the Olympic Games. The ranch across the highway from town usually has buffalo grazing by the fence. There are also deer, elk, and antelope. It is a good place to see these big animals up close.

Town Life

The people of Wright are very close to each other. Most people know everyone in town. Children have a lot of freedom because parents know that people are looking out for them. People in Wright enjoy watching the Panther sports teams. Many of the teams have won State Championships.

▼ A woman from the nearby Thunder Bay Coal Company's softball team practices her hitting. The company provides many activities for its workers.

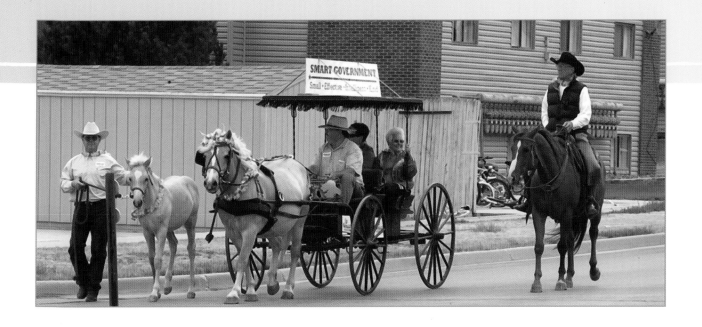

On Wright Days, there are street parades, farm shows, and tours at ranches. Everyone in the town watches or joins in the activities.

Every June, the town celebrates Wright Days. Everyone loves watching the parades. There are all kinds of activities to enjoy. Young children enter the fishing derby and visit the petting zoo. Many people join in the Fun Run and horseshoe **tournament**. Everyone is invited to the town barbecue.

A Mining Family

People who work in a mine have long **shifts**. A shift, or the time spent working, is usually 12 hours. The work at a mine never stops. This means workers sometimes sleep during the day and work at night. They all have to work some weekends and holidays, too.

▼ The Goodrich family moved from Michigan to Wyoming so that Zeb Goodrich, the father of the family, could work in the mine.

A miner climbs down from a giant coal shovel at the mine. His children miss him when he goes to work.

The coal mines of Wright are all surface mines. A large area of land is needed for surface mines, so they are set up a few miles away from the town. Buses take the workers from town to the mines and back again each day. This is helpful in winter when snow covers the road, making traveling difficult.

At the Mine

The Black Thunder coal mine near Wright is a surface mine with large **pits**. A mine is dug by first scraping away the **topsoil**. Under the topsoil is what miners call **overburden**. It is a mixture of ordinary rocks and soil. This is blasted away to get to the coal underneath. The topsoil and overburden are kept so that they can be used later to cover the mine when all the coal has been taken.

▼ Coal shovels are used to scoop out the coal from the mine.

Explosives shoot rocks and dust high into the air. Miners have to be very careful that they do not get hit when the rock is blasted.

Once the coal is uncovered, the miners start the main work. They first set explosives in the ground. When these go off, they loosen the coal. The miners then scoop up the coal with huge shovels. As the coal is taken away, the pit gets deeper and deeper until it becomes a giant hole in the ground.

Moving the Coal

After the coal has been mined, it is ready to go to the power plant. Loaders with large scoops or buckets load the coal onto coal-hauling trucks. These big trucks take the coal to a crusher. This breaks up big chunks of coal into small pieces. A **conveyor** then moves the coal to a storage **silo**.

▼ The coal mines in Wright have some of the biggest mine trucks in the world. The trucks are about 20 feet (6.5 meters) high and 54 feet (17 meters) long.

Railroads were built near the mines to transport the coal.

The silos hold the coal until it is loaded directly into railroad cars. These cars are large, open bins. The train stops under the silos so all the cars can be loaded. The train then takes the coal to a nearby power plant, where it is burned.

Reclaiming the Land

At some point, all mines run out of minerals and ores. **Laws** make sure mining **companies** think about what will happen when their mines are closed. The companies need to have a detailed plan for the land before they are allowed to start digging. This plan is known as a **reclamation** plan.

▼ New pine trees start to grow on land that was once a mine.

Grass seed is sprayed onto this closed mine. People try to return land that is no longer mined back to countryside.

Old machinery is taken away and garbage is cleaned up. Surface mines are sometimes filled in. The overburden that was set aside is brought back. It is used to help make the land level again. The topsoil is then spread over the top so plants will have good soil to grow in. Other mines are flooded to form lakes.

After the Mining

When a mine shuts down, the nearby town can become abandoned if there is no other work for the miners to do. The miners and their families begin to move away and their houses are either closed up or torn down. Stores close and schools become empty. The town soon turns into a ghost town.

▼ When the mine in Jeffrey City, Wyoming, shut down in 1982, most people left for the city in search of new work. The old mining town soon lost all its people and is now empty.

Power plants near Wright and the nearby town of Gillette are providing new jobs as mines close. Houses are being built for new people moving to the area.

In some places, people are finding new uses for empty mines. Because they are deep underground, it does not get very hot or cold. It stays the same temperature all year round. As long as the mine is not wet, it is a good place to store papers or grow mushrooms.

Mining Around the World

There are rural mining towns in many countries of the world. The coal-mining town of Barentsburg is on the remote island of Spitsbergen in the Arctic Ocean, in between Norway and Greenland. The coal is carried to other countries by ship.

▼ The coal mines in Barentsburg are right by the sea, making it easy to load the coal directly onto the ships.

A miner drills into the rock searching for emeralds in Colombia.

Colombia in South America is famous for its emeralds. These are found on the steep slopes of the mountains. Workers usually live in wooden huts perched on the mountainsides. The salt mine in Bochnia, Poland, is the oldest in the world. It contains many empty chambers and hallways. One large chamber is now used as a hospital for sick people.

Facts and Figures

Mining facts
The United States has a quarter of the world's reserves of coal. Most of that coal will be mined in surface mines. Canada is rich in oil and gas, as well as other minerals.

Mineral facts
There are more than 1,000 different minerals in the world. Only a few are common. Minerals are rated on a scale of hardness. Talc is the softest at 1, diamond the hardest at 10.

Ore facts
Ores are rocks or minerals that contain a metal that can easily be separated from it. Iron, lead, copper, mercury, and many other metals can all be found in ores.

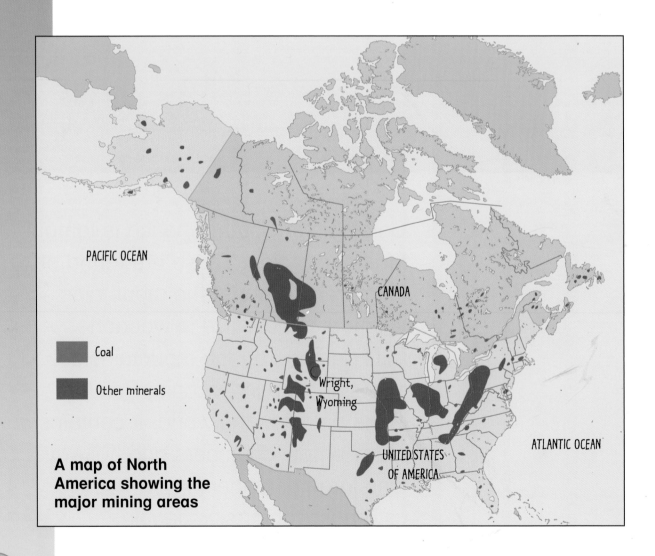

A map of North America showing the major mining areas

PACIFIC OCEAN

CANADA

Coal

Other minerals

Wright, Wyoming

UNITED STATES OF AMERICA

ATLANTIC OCEAN

Glossary

city The largest urban area, with thousands or millions of people and many stores, houses, schools, and factories

coal A black rock that burns and supplies heat and light

community A group of people who live, work, and play close together

company A group of people that work together to make, mine, or produce something

conveyor A long belt that moves things from one place to another

energy The power to do work, such as operate machines; energy can come from burning fuels such as coal, or from wind, water, and the Sun

explosive A chemical mixture that explodes and blows up the ground

law A rule made by the government of the country or area that must be obeyed by everyone in the area

metal A material that is usually hard and strong

mine To dig a hole or pit in the ground, called a mine, from which ores and minerals are dug out

mineral A substance that occurs naturally in rocks in the ground

mining Digging ores or minerals from the ground

ore A mineral that contains metal

overburden The rocks and dirt on top of the ore to be mined

pit A large hole in the ground

reclamation To restore something to good use

recreation center A place for community sports and activities

recycle To rework a mineral so that it can be used again in another form or another product

resources Things one needs or must have

rural A quiet living area in the countryside

shift One of several set periods of work during the day, often eight hours

silo A tall, round building for storing material

surface mine A mine in which the material to be mined lies close to the surface and is dug straight out

topsoil Surface soil good for growing plants

town A place where people live that has many houses, roads, and stores; small towns can be rural, large towns are urban

tournaments Games or contests

tunnel An underground passage in a mine

urban A built-up, busy area, such as a town or city

village A small rural place with a few houses

31

Further Information

Further Reading

Malam, John. *You Wouldn't Want to Be a 19th-Century Coal Miner in England!: A Dangerous Job You'd Rather Not Have.* Franklin Watts, 2006

Drake, Jane. *Mining.* Kids Can Press, Toronto, 1997

Matthews, Sheelagh. *Mining.* Weigl Educational Publishers, Calgary 2007

Ito, Tom. *The California Gold Rush.* Lucent Books, San Diego 1997

Web Sites

The Town of Wright
www.wrightwyoming.com

Mining
www.msha.gov/kids/mining.htm

Cariboo Gold Rush
bcheritage.ca/cariboo/contents.htm

Index

Printed in the U.S.A.—CG